The Homecoming

Harold Pinter was born in London in 1930. He is married to Antonia Fraser. In 1995 he was awarded the David Cohen British Literature Prize, for a lifetime's achievement in literature. In 1996 he was given the Laurence Olivier Award for a lifetime's achievement in theatre.

HAROLD PINTER

The Homecoming

faber and faber

First published in this edition in 1991
by Faber and Faber Limited
3 Queen Square London WC1N 3AU

Reprinted six times
Reset 1999
First published in 1965
by Eyre Methuen Ltd
Second edition 1966
Paperback edition first published in 1965
Reprinted by Methuen London Ltd in 1982
Reissued in 1986
Reprinted by Methuen Drama in 1988

Printed and bound in Great Britain by
Mackays of Chatham PLC, Chatham, Kent

All rights whatsoever in this play are strictly reserved
and application for performance etc., should be made in writing,
before rehearsals begin, to Judy Daish Associates,
2 St Charles Place, London W10 6EG

A CIP record for this book is available
from the British Library

ISBN 0-571-16080-8

8 10 9

Characters

MAX
a man of seventy

LENNY
a man in his early thirties

SAM
a man of sixty-three

JOEY
a man in his middle twenties

TEDDY
a man in his middle thirties

RUTH
a woman in her early thirties

The Homecoming was first presented by the Royal Shakespeare Company at the Aldwych Theatre on 3 June 1965, with the following cast:

MAX	Paul Rogers
LENNY	Ian Holm
SAM	John Normington
JOEY	Terence Rigby
TEDDY	Michael Bryant
RUTH	Vivien Merchant

Directed by Peter Hall

The play was presented by the Royal Shakespeare Company and Alexander H. Cohen at the Music Box Theatre, New York, on 5 January, 1967 with one change in the cast: the part of Teddy was played by Michael Craig.

The Homecoming was revived at the Garrick Theatre in May 1978. The cast was as follows:

MAX	Timothy West
RUTH	Gemma Jones
LENNY	Michael Kitchen
SAM	Charles Kay
JOEY	Roger Lloyd Pack
TEDDY	Oliver Cotton

Directed by Kevin Billington

The Homecoming was revived by The Peter Hall Company in association with Triumph Proscenium Productions Limited at the Comedy Theatre, London, on 9 January 1991 with the following cast:

MAX	Warren Mitchell
LENNY	Nicholas Woodeson
SAM	John Normington
JOEY	Douglas McFerran
TEDDY	Greg Hicks
RUTH	Cherie Lunghi

Directed by Peter Hall

Summer

An old house in North London.
A large room, extending the width of the stage.

The back wall, which contained the door, has been
removed. A square arch shape remains. Beyond it, the
hall. In the hall a staircase, ascending U.L.*, well in view.*
The front door U.R.*. A coatstand, hooks, etc.*

In the room a window, R*. Odd tables, chairs. Two*
large armchairs. A large sofa, L*. Against* R*. wall a large*
sideboard, the upper half of which contains a mirror.
U.L. *a radiogram.*

Act One

Evening.
LENNY is sitting on the sofa with a newspaper, a pencil in his hand. He wears a dark suit. He makes occasional marks on the back page.

MAX comes in, from the direction of the kitchen. He goes to sideboard, opens top drawer, rummages in it, closes it.

He wears an old cardigan and a cap, and carries a stick.

He walks downstage, stands, looks about the room.

MAX
What have you done with the scissors?

Pause.

I said I'm looking for the scissors. What have you done with them?

Pause.

Did you hear me? I want to cut something out of the paper.

LENNY
I'm reading the paper.

MAX

Not that paper. I haven't even read that paper. I'm
talking about last Sunday's paper. I was just having a
look at it in the kitchen.

Pause.

Do you hear what I'm saying? I'm talking to you!
Where's the scissors?

LENNY
(*looking up, quietly*)
Why don't you shut up, you daft prat?

MAX *lifts his stick and points it at him.*

MAX

Don't you talk to me like that. I'm warning you.

He sits in large armchair.

There's an advertisement in the paper about flannel vests.
Cut price. Navy surplus. I could do with a few of them.

Pause.

I think I'll have a fag. Give me a fag.

Pause.

I just asked you to give me a cigarette.

Pause.

4

Look what I'm lumbered with.

He takes a crumpled cigarette from his pocket.

I'm getting old, my word of honour.

He lights it.

You think I wasn't a tearaway? I could have taken care of you, twice over. I'm still strong. You ask your Uncle Sam what I was. But at the same time I always had a kind heart. Always.

Pause.

I used to knock about with a man called MacGregor. I called him Mac. You remember Mac? Eh?

Pause.

Huhh! We were two of the worst hated men in the West End of London. I tell you, I still got the scars. We'd walk into a place, the whole room'd stand up, they'd make way to let us pass. You never heard such silence. Mind you, he was a big man, he was over six foot tall. His family were all MacGregors, they came all the way from Aberdeen, but he was the only one they called Mac.

Pause.

He was very fond of your mother, Mac was. Very fond. He always had a good word for her.

Pause.

Mind you, she wasn't such a bad woman. Even though it made me sick just to look at her rotten stinking face, she wasn't such a bad bitch. I gave her the best bleeding years of my life, anyway.

LENNY

Plug it, will you, you stupid sod, I'm trying to read the paper.

MAX

Listen! I'll chop your spine off, you talk to me like that! You understand? Talking to your lousy filthy father like that!

LENNY

You know what, you're getting demented.

Pause.

What do you think of Second Wind for the three-thirty?

MAX

Where?

LENNY

Sandown Park.

MAX

Don't stand a chance.

LENNY

Sure he does.

MAX

Not a chance.

LENNY

He's the winner.

LENNY *ticks the paper.*

MAX

He talks to me about horses.

Pause.

I used to live on the course. One of the loves of my life.
Epsom? I knew it like the back of my hand. I was one of
the best-known faces down at the paddock. What a
marvellous open-air life.

Pause.

He talks to me about horses. You only read their names
in the papers. But I've stroked their manes, I've held
them, I've calmed them down before a big race. I was
the one they used to call for. Max, they'd say, there's a
horse here, he's highly strung, you're the only man on
the course who can calm him. It was true. I had a . . . I
had an instinctive understanding of animals. I should
have been a trainer. Many times I was offered the job –
you know, a proper post, by the Duke of . . . I forget his
name . . . one of the Dukes. But I had family
obligations, my family needed me at home.

7

Pause.

The times I've watched those animals thundering past the post. What an experience. Mind you, I didn't lose, I made a few bob out of it, and you know why? Because I always had the smell of a good horse. I could smell him. And not only the colts but the fillies. Because the fillies are more highly strung than the colts, they're more unreliable, did you know that? No, what do you know? Nothing. But I was always able to tell a good filly by one particular trick. I'd look her in the eye. You see? I'd stand in front of her and look her straight in the eye, it was a kind of hypnotism, and by the look deep down in her eye I could tell whether she was a stayer or not. It was a gift. I had a gift.

Pause.

And he talks to me about horses.

LENNY

Dad, do you mind if I change the subject?

Pause.

I want to ask you something. The dinner we had before, what was the name of it? What do you call it?

Pause.

Why don't you buy a dog? You're a dog cook. Honest. You think you're cooking for a lot of dogs.

8

MAX

If you don't like it get out.

LENNY

I am going out. I'm going out to buy myself a proper
dinner.

MAX

Well, get out! What are you waiting for?

LENNY *looks at him.*

LENNY

What did you say?

MAX

I said shove off out of it, that's what I said.

LENNY

You'll go before me, Dad, if you talk to me in that tone
of voice.

MAX

Will I, you bitch?

MAX *grips his stick.*

LENNY

Oh, Daddy, you're not going to use your stick on me,
are you? Eh? Don't use your stick on me Daddy. No,
please. It wasn't my fault, it was one of the others. I
haven't done anything wrong, Dad, honest. Don't clout
me with that stick, Dad.

Silence.

MAX *sits hunched.* LENNY *reads the paper.*

SAM *comes in the front door. He wears a chauffeur's uniform. He hangs his hat on a hook in the hall and comes into the room. He goes to a chair, sits in it and sighs.*

Hullo, Uncle Sam.

SAM

Hullo.

LENNY

How are you, Uncle?

SAM

Not bad. A bit tired.

LENNY

Tired? I bet you're tired. Where you been?

SAM

I've been to London Airport.

LENNY

All the way up to London Airport? What, right up the M4?

SAM

Yes, all the way up there.

LENNY

Tch, tch, tch. Well, I think you're entitled to be tired, Uncle.

SAM

Well, it's the drivers.

LENNY

I know. That's what I'm talking about. I'm talking about the drivers.

SAM

Knocks you out.

Pause.

MAX

I'm here, too, you know.

SAM *looks at him.*

I said I'm here, too. I'm sitting here.

SAM

I know you're here.

Pause.

SAM

I took a Yankee out there today . . . to the Airport.

LENNY

Oh, a Yankee, was it?

SAM

Yes, I been with him all day. Picked him up at the Savoy at half past twelve, took him to the Caprice for his lunch. After lunch I picked him up again, took him down to a house in Eaton Square – he had to pay a visit to a friend there – and then round about tea-time I took him right the way out to the Airport.

LENNY

Had to catch a plane there, did he?

SAM

Yes. Look what he gave me. He gave me a box of cigars.

SAM *takes a box of cigars from his pocket.*

MAX

Come here. Let's have a look at them.

SAM *shows* MAX *the cigars.* MAX *takes one from the box, pinches it and sniffs it.*

It's a fair cigar.

SAM

Want to try one?

MAX *and* SAM *light cigars.*

You know what he said to me? He told me I was the best chauffeur he'd ever had. The best one.

MAX

From what point of view?

SAM

Eh?

MAX

From what point of view?

LENNY

From the point of view of his driving, Dad, and his
general sense of courtesy, I should say.

MAX

Thought you were a good driver, did he, Sam? Well, he
gave you a first-class cigar.

SAM

Yes, he thought I was the best he'd ever had. They all
say that, you know. They won't have anyone else, they
only ask for me. They say I'm the best chauffeur in the
firm.

LENNY

I bet the other drivers tend to get jealous, don't they,
Uncle?

SAM

They do get jealous. They get very jealous.

MAX

Why?

13

Pause.

I just told you.

MAX

No, I just can't get it clear, Sam. Why do the other drivers get jealous?

SAM

Because (a) I'm the best driver, and because . . . (b) I don't take liberties.

Pause.

I don't press myself on people, you see. These big businessmen, men of affairs, they don't want the driver jawing all the time, they like to sit in the back, have a bit of peace and quiet. After all, they're sitting in a Humber Super Snipe, they can afford to relax. At the same time, though, this is what really makes me special . . . I do know how to pass the time of day when required.

Pause.

For instance, I told this man today I was in the second world war. Not the first. I told him I was too young for the first. But I told him I fought in the second.

Pause.

So did he, it turned out.

LENNY *stands, goes to the mirror and straightens his tie.*

LENNY

He was probably a colonel, or something, in the American Air Force.

SAM

Yes.

LENNY

Probably a navigator, or something like that, in a Flying Fortress. Now he's most likely a high executive in a worldwide group of aeronautical engineers.

SAM

Yes.

LENNY

Yes, I know the kind of man you're talking about.

LENNY *goes out, turning to his right.*

SAM

After all, I'm experienced. I was driving a dust cart at the age of nineteen. Then I was in long-distance haulage. I had ten years as a taxi-driver and I've had five as a private chauffeur.

MAX

It's funny you never got married, isn't it? A man with all your gifts.

Pause.

Isn't it? A man like you?

SAM

There's still time.

MAX

Is there?

Pause.

SAM

You'd be surprised.

MAX

What you been doing, banging away at your lady
customers, have you?

SAM

Not me.

MAX

In the back of the Snipe? Been having a few crafty reefs
in a layby, have you?

SAM

Not me.

MAX

On the back seat? What about the armrest, was it up or
down?

SAM

I've never done that kind of thing in my car.

MAX

Above all that kind of thing, are you, Sam?

SAM

Too true.

MAX

Above having a good bang on the back seat, are you?

SAM

Yes, I leave that to others.

MAX

You leave it to others? What others? You paralysed prat!

SAM

I don't mess up my car! Or my . . . my boss's car! Like other people.

MAX

Other people? What other people?

Pause.

What other people?

Pause.

SAM

Other people.

Pause.

MAX

When you find the right girl, Sam, let your family know, don't forget, we'll give you a number one send-off, I promise you. You can bring her to live here, she can keep us all happy. We'd take it in turns to give her a walk round the park.

SAM

I wouldn't bring her here.

MAX

Sam, it's your decision. You're welcome to bring your bride here, to the place where you live, or on the other hand you can take a suite at the Dorchester. It's entirely up to you.

SAM

I haven't got a bride.

SAM *stands, goes to the sideboard, takes an apple from the bowl, bites into it.*

Getting a bit peckish.

He looks out of the window.

Never get a bride like you had, anyway. Nothing like your bride . . . going about these days. Like Jessie.

Pause.

After all, I escorted her once or twice, didn't I? Drove her round once or twice in my cab. She was a charming woman.

Pause.

All the same, she was your wife. But still . . . they were some of the most delightful evenings I've ever had. Used to just drive her about. It was my pleasure.

MAX
(*softly, closing his eyes*)

Christ.

SAM

I used to pull up at a stall and buy her a cup of coffee. She was a very nice companion to be with.

Silence.

JOEY *comes in the front door. He walks into the room, takes his jacket off, throws it on a chair and stands.*

Silence.

JOEY

Feel a bit hungry.

SAM

Me, too.

19

MAX

Who do you think I am, your mother? Eh? Honest.
They walk in here every time of the day and night like
bloody animals. Go and find yourself a mother.

LENNY *walks into the room, stands.*

JOEY

I've been training down at the gym.

SAM

Yes, the boy's been working all day and training all
night.

MAX

What do you want, you bitch? You spend all the day
sitting on your arse at London Airport, buy yourself a
jamroll. You expect me to sit here waiting to rush into
the kitchen the moment you step in the door? You've
been living sixty-three years, why don't you learn to
cook?

SAM

I can cook.

MAX

Well, go and cook!

Pause.

LENNY

What the boys want, Dad, is your own special brand of
cooking, Dad. That's what the boys look forward to.

The special understanding of food, you know, that
you've got.

                              MAX

Stop calling me Dad. Just stop all that calling me Dad,
do you understand?

                            LENNY

But I'm your son. You used to tuck me up in bed every
night. He tucked you up, too, didn't he, Joey?

Pause.

He used to like tucking up his sons.

LENNY *turns and goes towards the front door.*

                              MAX

Lenny.

                            LENNY
                          (*turning*)

What?

                              MAX

I'll give you a proper tuck up one of these nights, son.
You mark my word.

They look at each other.

LENNY *opens the front door and goes out.*

Silence.

JOEY

I've been training with Bobby Dodd.

Pause.

And I had a good go at the bag as well.

Pause.

I wasn't in bad trim.

MAX

Boxing's a gentleman's game.

Pause.

I'll tell you what you've got to do. What you've got to do is you've got to learn how to defend yourself, and you've got to learn how to attack. That's your only trouble as a boxer. You don't know how to defend yourself, and you don't know how to attack.

Pause.

Once you've mastered those arts you can go straight to the top.

Pause.

JOEY

I've got a pretty good idea . . . of how to do that.

JOEY *looks round for his jacket, picks it up, goes out of the room and up the stairs.*

Pause.

MAX

Sam . . . why don't you go, too, eh? Why don't you just go upstairs? Leave me quiet. Leave me alone.

SAM

I want to make something clear about Jessie, Max. I want to. I do. When I took her out in the cab, round the town, I was taking care of her, for you. I was looking after her for you, when you were busy, wasn't I? I was showing her the West End.

Pause.

You wouldn't have trusted any of your other brothers. You wouldn't have trusted Mac, would you? But you trusted me. I want to remind you.

Pause.

Old Mac died a few years ago, didn't he? Isn't he dead?

Pause.

He was a lousy stinking rotten loudmouth. A bastard uncouth sodding runt. Mind you, he was a good friend of yours.

Pause.

MAX

Eh, Sam . . .

SAM

What?

MAX

Why do I keep you here? You're just an old grub.

SAM

Am I?

MAX

You're a maggot.

SAM

Oh yes?

MAX

As soon as you stop paying your way here, I mean when you're too old to pay your way, you know what I'm going to do? I'm going to give you the boot.

SAM

You are, eh?

MAX

Sure. I mean, bring in the money and I'll put up with you. But when the firm gets rid of you – you can flake off.

SAM

This is my house as well, you know. This was our mother's house.

24

One lot after the other. One mess after the other.

Our father's house.

Look what I'm lumbered with. One cast-iron bunch of crap after another. One flow of stinking pus after another.

Pause.

Our father! I remember him. Don't worry. You kid yourself. He used to come over to me and look down at me. My old man did. He'd bend right over me, then he'd pick me up. I was only that big. Then he'd dandle me. Give me the bottle. Wipe me clean. Give me a smile. Pat me on the bum. Pass me around, pass me from hand to hand. Toss me up in the air. Catch me coming down. I remember my father.

BLACKOUT.

LIGHTS UP.

Night.

TEDDY *and* RUTH *stand at the threshold of the room. They are both well dressed in light summer suits and light raincoats.*

Two suitcases are by their side.

25

They look at the room. TEDDY *tosses the key in his hand, smiles.*

TEDDY

Well, the key worked.

Pause.

They haven't changed the lock.

Pause.

RUTH

No one's here.

TEDDY
(*looking up*)

They're asleep.

Pause.

RUTH

Can I sit down?

TEDDY

Of course.

RUTH

I'm tired.

Pause.

Then sit down.

She does not move.

That's my father's chair.

RUTH
That one?

TEDDY
(*smiling*)
Yes, that's it. Shall I go up and see if my room's still there?

RUTH
It can't have moved.

TEDDY
No, I mean if my bed's still there.

RUTH
Someone might be in it.

TEDDY
No. They've got their own beds.

Pause.

RUTH
Shouldn't you wake someone up? Tell them you're here?

Not at this time of night. It's too late.

Pause.

Shall I go up?

He goes into the hall, looks up the stairs, comes back.

Why don't you sit down?

Pause.

I'll just go up . . . have a look.

He goes up the stairs, stealthily.

RUTH *stands, then slowly walks across the room.*

TEDDY *returns.*

It's still there. My room. Empty. The bed's there. What are you doing?

She looks at him.

Blankets, no sheets. I'll find some sheets. I could hear snores. Really. They're all still here, I think. They're all snoring up there. Are you cold?

RUTH

No.

TEDDY

I'll make something to drink, if you like. Something hot.

RUTH

No, I don't want anything.

TEDDY *walks about.*

TEDDY

What do you think of the room? Big, isn't it? It's a big
house. I mean, it's a fine room, don't you think?
Actually there was a wall, across there . . . with a door.
We knocked it down . . . years ago . . . to make an
open living area. The structure wasn't affected, you see.
My mother was dead.

RUTH *sits.*

Tired?

RUTH

Just a little.

TEDDY

We can go to bed if you like. No point in waking
anyone up now. Just go to bed. See them all in the
morning . . . see my father in the morning . . .

Pause.

RUTH

Do you want to stay?

29

TEDDY

Stay?

Pause.

We've come to stay. We're bound to stay . . . for a few days.

RUTH

I think . . . the children . . . might be missing us.

TEDDY

Don't be silly.

RUTH

They might.

TEDDY

Look, we'll be back in a few days, won't we?

He walks about the room.

Nothing's changed. Still the same.

Pause.

Still, he'll get a surprise in the morning, won't he? The old man. I think you'll like him very much. Honestly. He's a . . . well, he's old, of course. Getting on.

Pause.

I was born here, do you realize that?

30

RUTH

I know.

Pause.

TEDDY

Why don't you go to bed? I'll find some sheets. I feel
. . . wide awake, isn't it odd? I think I'll stay up for a
bit. Are you tired?

RUTH

No.

TEDDY

Go to bed. I'll show you the room.

RUTH

No, I don't want to.

TEDDY

You'll be perfectly all right up there without me. Really
you will. I mean, I won't be long. Look, it's just up
there. It's the first door on the landing. The bathroom's
right next door. You . . . need some rest, you know.

Pause.

I just want to . . . walk about for a few minutes. Do you
mind?

RUTH

Of course I don't.

31

TEDDY

Well . . . Shall I show you the room?

RUTH

No, I'm happy at the moment.

TEDDY

You don't have to go to bed. I'm not saying you have
to. I mean, you can stay up with me. Perhaps I'll make a
cup of tea or something. The only thing is we don't
want to make too much noise, we don't want to wake
anyone up.

RUTH

I'm not making any noise.

TEDDY

I know you're not.

He goes to her.

(*gently*)
Look, it's all right, really. I'm here. I mean . . . I'm with
you. There's no need to be nervous. Are you nervous?

RUTH

No.

TEDDY

There's no need to be.

Pause.

They're very warm people, really. Very warm. They're
my family. They're not ogres.

Pause.

Well, perhaps we should go to bed. After all, we have to
be up early, see Dad. Wouldn't be quite right if he found
us in bed, I think.
                    (*he chuckles.*)
Have to be up before six, come down, say hullo.

Pause.

                    RUTH
I think I'll have a breath of air.

                    TEDDY
Air?

Pause.

What do you mean?

                    RUTH
                  (*standing*)
Just a stroll.

                    TEDDY
At this time of night? But we've . . . only just got here.
We've got to go to bed.

                    RUTH
I just feel like some air.

TEDDY

But I'm going to bed.

RUTH

That's all right.

TEDDY

But what am I going to do?

Pause.

The last thing I want is a breath of air. Why do you
want a breath of air?

RUTH

I just do.

TEDDY

But it's late.

RUTH

I won't go far. I'll come back.

Pause.

TEDDY

I'll wait up for you.

RUTH

Why?

TEDDY

I'm not going to bed without you.

34

Can I have the key?

He gives it to her.

Why don't you go to bed?

He puts his arms on her shoulders and kisses her. They look at each other, briefly. She smiles.

I won't be long.

She goes out of the front door.

TEDDY *goes to the window, peers out after her, half turns from the window, stands, suddenly chews his knuckles.*

LENNY *walks into the room from* U.L. *He stands. He wears pyjamas and dressing-gown. He watches* TEDDY.

TEDDY *turns and sees him.*

Silence.

TEDDY

Hullo, Lenny.

LENNY

Hullo, Teddy.

Pause.

TEDDY

I didn't hear you come down the stairs.

LENNY

I didn't.

Pause.

I sleep down here now. Next door. I've got a kind of study, workroom cum bedroom next door now, you see.

TEDDY

Oh. Did I . . . wake you up?

LENNY

No. I just had an early night tonight. You know how it is. Can't sleep. Keep waking up.

Pause.

TEDDY

How are you?

LENNY

Well, just sleeping a bit restlessly, that's all. Tonight, anyway.

TEDDY

Bad dreams?

LENNY

No, I wouldn't say I was dreaming. It's not exactly a

dream. It's just that something keeps waking me up. Some kind of tick.

TEDDY

A tick?

LENNY

Yes.

TEDDY

Well, what is it?

LENNY

I don't know.

Pause.

TEDDY

Have you got a clock in your room?

LENNY

Yes.

TEDDY

Well, maybe it's the clock.

LENNY

Yes, could be, I suppose.

Pause.

Well, if it's the clock I'd better do something about it, stifle it in some way, or something.

37

Pause.

TEDDY

I've . . . just come back for a few days.

LENNY

Oh yes? Have you?

Pause.

TEDDY

How's the old man?

LENNY

He's in the pink.

Pause.

TEDDY

I've been keeping well.

LENNY

Oh, have you?

Pause.

Staying the night then, are you?

TEDDY

Yes.

LENNY

Well, you can sleep in your old room.

TEDDY

Yes, I've been up.

LENNY

Yes, you can sleep there.

LENNY *yawns*.

Oh well.

TEDDY

I'm going to bed.

LENNY

Are you?

TEDDY

Yes, I'll get some sleep.

LENNY

Yes I'm going to bed, too.

TEDDY *picks up the cases*.

I'll give you a hand.

TEDDY

No, they're not heavy.

TEDDY *goes into the hall with the cases*.

LENNY *turns out the light in the room*.

39

The light in the hall remains on.

LENNY *follows into the hall.*

LENNY

Nothing you want?

TEDDY

Mmmm?

LENNY

Nothing you might want, for the night? Glass of water, anything like that?

TEDDY

Any sheets anywhere?

LENNY

In the sideboard in your room.

TEDDY

Oh, good.

LENNY

Friends of mine occasionally stay there, you know, in your room, when they're passing through this part of the world.

LENNY *turns out the hall light and turns on the first landing light.*

TEDDY *begins to walk up the stairs.*

TEDDY

Well, I'll see you at breakfast, then.

LENNY

Yes, that's it. Ta-ta.

TEDDY *goes upstairs.*

LENNY *goes off* L.

Silence.

The landing light goes out.

Slight night light in the hall and room.

LENNY *comes back into the room, goes to the window and looks out.*

He leaves the window and turns on a lamp.

He is holding a small clock.

He sits, places the clock in front of him, lights a cigarette and sits.

RUTH *comes in the front door.*

She stands still. LENNY *turns his head, smiles. She walks slowly into the room.*

LENNY

Good evening.

RUTH

Morning, I think.

LENNY

You're right there.

Pause.

My name's Lenny. What's yours?

RUTH

Ruth.

She sits, puts her coat collar around her.

LENNY

Cold?

RUTH

No.

LENNY

It's been a wonderful summer, hasn't it? Remarkable.

Pause.

Would you like something? Refreshment of some kind? An aperitif, anything like that?

RUTH

No, thanks.

I'm glad you said that. We haven't got a drink in the
house. Mind you, I'd soon get some in, if we had a
party or something like that. Some kind of celebration
. . . you know.

Pause.

You must be connected with my brother in some way.
The one who's been abroad.

RUTH

I'm his wife.

LENNY

Eh listen, I wonder if you can advise me. I've been
having a bit of a rough time with this clock. The tick's
been keeping me up. The trouble is I'm not all that
convinced it was the clock. I mean there are lots of
things which tick in the night, don't you find that? All
sorts of objects, which, in the day, you wouldn't call
anything else but commonplace. They give you no
trouble. But in the night any given one of a number of
them is liable to start letting out a bit of a tick. Whereas
you look at these objects in the day and they're just
commonplace. They're as quiet as mice during the
daytime. So . . . all things being equal . . . this question
of me saying it was the clock that woke me up, well,
that could very easily prove something of a false
hypothesis.

*He goes to the sideboard, pours from a jug into a glass,
takes the glass to* RUTH.

43

Here you are. I bet you could do with this.

What is it?

Water.

She takes it, sips, places the glass on a small table by her chair.

LENNY *watches her.*

Isn't it funny? I've got my pyjamas on and you're fully dressed.

He goes to the sideboard and pours another glass of water.

Mind if I have one? Yes, it's funny seeing my old brother again after all these years. It's just the sort of tonic my Dad needs, you know. He'll be chuffed to his bollocks in the morning, when he sees his eldest son. I was surprised myself when I saw Teddy, you know. Old Ted. I thought he was in America.

We're on a visit to Europe.

What, both of you?

RUTH

Yes.

LENNY

What, you sort of live with him over there, do you?

RUTH

We're married.

LENNY

On a visit to Europe, eh? Seen much of it?

RUTH

We've just come from Italy.

LENNY

Oh, you went to Italy first, did you? And then he brought you over here to meet the family, did he? Well, the old man'll be pleased to see you, I can tell you.

RUTH

Good.

LENNY

What did you say?

RUTH

Good.

Pause.

LENNY

Where'd you go to in Italy?

45

RUTH

Venice.

LENNY

Not dear old Venice? Eh? That's funny. You know, I've
always had a feeling that if I'd been a soldier in the last
war – say in the Italian campaign – I'd probably have
found myself in Venice. I've always had that feeling.
The trouble was I was too young to serve, you see. I
was only a child, I was too small, otherwise I've got a
pretty shrewd idea I'd probably have gone through
Venice. Yes, I'd almost certainly have gone through it
with my battalion. Do you mind if I hold your hand?

RUTH

Why?

LENNY

Just a touch.

He stands and goes to her.

Just a tickle.

RUTH

Why?

He looks down at her.

LENNY

I'll tell you why.

Slight pause.

46

One night, not too long ago, one night down by the docks, I was standing alone under an arch, watching all the men jibbing the boom, out in the harbour, and playing about with a yardarm, when a certain lady came up to me and made me a certain proposal. This lady had been searching for me for days. She'd lost tracks of my whereabouts. However, the fact was she eventually caught up with me, and when she caught up with me she made me this certain proposal. Well, this proposal wasn't entirely out of order and normally I would have subscribed to it. I mean I would have subscribed to it in the normal course of events. The only trouble was she was falling apart with the pox. So I turned it down. Well, this lady was very insistent and started taking liberties with me down under this arch, liberties which by any criterion I couldn't be expected to tolerate, the facts being what they were, so I clumped her one. It was on my mind at the time to do away with her, you know, to kill her, and the fact is, that as killings go, it would have been a simple matter, nothing to it. Her chauffeur, who had located me for her, he'd popped round the corner to have a drink, which just left this lady and myself, you see, alone, standing underneath this arch, watching all the steamers steaming up, no one about, all quiet on the Western Front, and there she was up against this wall – well, just sliding down the wall, following the blow I'd given her. Well, to sum up, everything was in my favour, for a killing. Don't worry about the chauffeur. The chauffeur would never have spoken. He was an old friend of the family. But . . . in the end I thought . . . Aaah, why go to all the bother . . . you know, getting rid of the corpse and all that, getting yourself into a state of tension. So I just gave her another belt in the nose and a couple of turns of the boot and sort of left it at that.

RUTH

How did you know she was diseased?

LENNY

How did I know?

Pause.

I decided she was.

Silence.

You and my brother are newly-weds, are you?

RUTH

We've been married six years.

LENNY

He's always been my favourite brother, old Teddy. Do you know that? And my goodness we are proud of him here, I can tell you. Doctor of Philosophy and all that . . . leaves quite an impression. Of course, he's a very sensitive man, isn't he? Ted. Very. I've often wished I was as sensitive as he is.

RUTH

Have you?

LENNY

Oh yes. Oh yes, very much so. I mean, I'm not saying

48

I'm not sensitive. I am. I could just be a bit more so, that's all.

Could you?

Yes, just a bit more so, that's all.

Pause.

I mean, I am very sensitive to atmosphere, but I tend to get desensitized, if you know what I mean, when people make unreasonable demands on me. For instance, last Christmas I decided to do a bit of snow-clearing for the Borough Council, because we had a heavy snow over here that year in Europe. I didn't have to do this snow-clearing – I mean I wasn't financially embarrassed in any way – it just appealed to me, it appealed to something inside me. What I anticipated with a good deal of pleasure was the brisk cold bite in the air in the early morning. And I was right. I had to get my snowboots on and I had to stand on a corner, at about five-thirty in the morning, to wait for the lorry to pick me up, to take me to the allotted area. Bloody freezing. Well, the lorry came, I jumped on the tailboard, headlights on, dipped, and off we went. Got there, shovels up, fags on, and off we went, deep into the December snow, hours before cockcrow. Well, that morning, while I was having my mid-morning cup of tea in a neighbouring cafe, the shovel standing by my chair, an old lady approached me and asked me if I would give her a hand with her iron mangle. Her brother-in-law, she said, had left it for her, but he'd left it in the wrong room, he'd left it in the front room. Well, naturally, she wanted it in the back room. It was a present he'd given her, you see, a mangle, to iron out the washing. But he'd left it in the wrong room, he'd left it in the front room, well that was a silly place to leave it, it couldn't stay there. So I took time off to give her a hand. She only lived up the road. Well, the only trouble was when I got there I couldn't move this mangle. It must have weighed about half a ton. How this brother-in-law got it up there in the first place I can't even begin to envisage. So there I was, doing a bit of shoulders on with the mangle, risking a rupture, and this old lady just standing there, waving me on, not even lifting a little finger to give me a helping hand. So after a few minutes I said to her, now look here, why don't you stuff this iron mangle up your arse? Anyway, I said, they're out of date, you want to get a spin drier. I had a good mind to give her a workover there and then, but as I was feeling jubilant with the snow-clearing I just gave her a short-arm jab to the belly and jumped on a bus outside. Excuse me, shall I take this ashtray out of your way?

RUTH

It's not in my way.

LENNY

It seems to be in the way of your glass. The glass was about to fall. Or the ashtray. I'm rather worried about the carpet. It's not me, it's my father. He's obsessed with order and clarity. He doesn't like mess. So, as I don't believe you're smoking at the moment, I'm sure you won't object if I move the ashtray.

50

He does so.

And now perhaps I'll relieve you of your glass.

RUTH

I haven't quite finished.

LENNY

You've consumed quite enough, in my opinion.

RUTH

No, I haven't.

LENNY

Quite sufficient, in my own opinion.

RUTH

Not in mine, Leonard.

Pause.

LENNY

Don't call me that, please.

RUTH

Why not?

LENNY

That's the name my mother gave me.

Pause.

Just give me the glass.

51

RUTH

No.

Pause.

LENNY

I'll take it, then.

RUTH

If you take the glass . . . I'll take you.

Pause.

LENNY

How about me taking the glass without you taking me?

RUTH

Why don't I just take you?

Pause.

LENNY

You're joking.

Pause.

You're in love, anyway, with another man. You've had a secret liaison with another man. His family didn't even know. Then you come here without a word of warning and start to make trouble.

She picks up the glass and lifts it towards him.

RUTH

Have a sip. Go on. Have a sip from my glass.

He is still.

Sit on my lap. Take a long cool sip.

She pats her lap. Pause.

She stands, moves to him with the glass.

Put your head back and open your mouth.

LENNY

Take that glass away from me.

RUTH

Lie on the floor. Go on. I'll pour it down your throat.

LENNY

What are you doing, making me some kind of
proposal?

She laughs shortly, drains the glass.

RUTH

Oh, I was thirsty.

*She smiles at him, puts the glass down, goes into the
hall and up the stairs.*

LENNY

What was that supposed to be? Some kind of proposal?

Silence.

He comes back into the room, goes to his own glass, drains it.

A door slams upstairs.

The landing light goes on.

MAX *comes down the stairs, in pyjamas and cap. He comes into the room.*

MAX

What's going on here? You drunk?

He stares at LENNY.

What are you shouting about? You gone mad?

LENNY *pours another glass of water.*

Prancing about in the middle of the night shouting your head off. What are you, a raving lunatic?

LENNY

I was thinking aloud.

MAX

Is Joey down here? You been shouting at Joey?

LENNY

Didn't you hear what I said, Dad? I said I was thinking aloud.

MAX

You were thinking so loud you got me out of bed.

LENNY

Look, why don't you just . . . pop off, eh?

MAX

Pop off? He wakes me up in the middle of the night, I think we got burglars here, I think he's got a knife stuck in him, I come down here, he tells me to pop off.

LENNY *sits down.*

He was talking to someone. Who could he have been talking to? They're all asleep. He was having a conversation with someone. He won't tell me who it was. He pretends he was thinking aloud. What are you doing, hiding someone here?

LENNY

I was sleepwalking. Get out of it, leave me alone, will you?

MAX

I want an explanation, you understand? I asked you who you got hiding here.

Pause.

LENNY

I'll tell you what, Dad, since you're in the mood for a bit of a . . . chat, I'll ask you a question. It's a question I've been meaning to ask you for some time. That night . . . you know . . . the night you got me . . . that night

55

with Mum, what was it like? Eh? When I was just a
glint in your eye. What was it like? What was the
background to it? I mean, I want to know the real facts
about my background. I mean, for instance, is it a fact
that you had me in mind all the time, or is it a fact that I
was the last thing you had in mind?

Pause.

I'm only asking this in a spirit of inquiry, you
understand that, don't you? I'm curious. And there's
lots of people of my age share that curiosity, you know
that, Dad? They often ruminate, sometimes singly,
sometimes in groups, about the true facts of that
particular night – the night they were made in the image
of those two people *at it*. It's a question long overdue,
from my point of view, but as we happen to be passing
the time of day here tonight I thought I'd pop it to you.

Pause.

MAX

You'll drown in your own blood.

LENNY

If you prefer to answer the question in writing I've got
no objection.

MAX *stands*.

I should have asked my dear mother. Why didn't I ask
my dear mother? Now it's too late. She's passed over to
the other side.

MAX *spits at him.*

LENNY *looks down at the carpet.*

Now look what you've done. I'll have to Hoover that in the morning, you know.

MAX *turns and walks up the stairs.*

LENNY *sits still.*

BLACKOUT.

LIGHTS UP.

Morning.

JOEY *in front of the mirror. He is doing some slow limbering-up exercises. He stops, combs his hair, carefully. He then shadowboxes, heavily, watching himself in the mirror.*

MAX *comes in from* U.L.

Both MAX *and* JOEY *are dressed.* MAX *watches* JOEY *in silence.* JOEY *stops shadowboxing, picks up a newspaper and sits.*

Silence.

                    MAX
I hate this room.

Pause.

It's the kitchen I like. It's nice in there. It's cosy.

Pause.

But I can't stay in there. You know why? Because he's always washing up in there, scraping the plates, driving me out of the kitchen, that's why.

JOEY
Why don't you bring your tea in here?

MAX
I don't want to bring my tea in here. I hate it here. I want to drink my tea in there.

He goes into the hall and looks towards the kitchen.

What's he doing in there?

He returns.

What's the time?

JOEY
Half past six.

MAX
Half past six.

Pause.

I'm going to see a game of football this afternoon. You
want to come?

Pause.

I'm talking to you.

JOEY

I'm training this afternoon. I'm doing six rounds with
Blackie.

MAX

That's not till five o'clock. You've got time to see a
game of football before five o'clock. It's the first game of
the season.

JOEY

No, I'm not going.

MAX

Why not?

Pause.

MAX *goes into the hall.*

Sam! Come here!

MAX *comes back into the room.*

SAM *enters with a cloth.*

SAM

What?

MAX

What are you doing in there?

SAM

Washing up.

MAX

What else?

SAM

Getting rid of your leavings.

MAX

Putting them in the bin, eh?

SAM

Right in.

MAX

What point you trying to prove?

SAM

No point.

MAX

Oh yes, you are. You resent making my breakfast, that's
what it is, isn't it? That's why you bang round the
kitchen like that, scraping the frying-pan, scraping all
the leavings into the bin, scraping all the plates,

scraping all the tea out of the teapot . . . that's why you
do that, every single stinking morning. I know. Listen,
Sam. I want to say something to you. From my heart.

He moves closer.

I want you to get rid of these feelings of resentment
you've got towards me. I wish I could understand them.
Honestly, have I ever given you cause? Never. When
Dad died he said to me, Max, look after your brothers.
That's exactly what he said to me.

SAM

How could he say that when he was dead?

MAX

What?

SAM

How could he speak if he was dead?

Pause.

MAX

Before he died, Sam. Just before. They were his last
words. His last sacred words, Sammy. You think I'm
joking? You think when my father spoke – on his
deathbed – I wouldn't obey his words to the last letter?
You hear that, Joey? He'll stop at nothing. He's even
prepared to spit on the memory of our Dad. What kind
of a son were you, you wet wick? You spent half your
time doing crossword puzzles! We took you into the
butcher's shop, you couldn't even sweep the dust off

the floor. We took MacGregor into the shop, he could run the place by the end of a week. Well, I'll tell you one thing. I respected my father not only as a man but as a number one butcher! And to prove it I followed him into the shop. I learned to carve a carcass at his knee. I commemorated his name in blood. I gave birth to three grown men! All on my own bat. What have you done?

Pause.

What have you done? You tit!

SAM

Do you want to finish the washing up? Look, here's the cloth.

MAX

So try to get rid of these feelings of resentment, Sam. After all, we are brothers.

SAM

Do you want the cloth? Here you are. Take it.

TEDDY *and* RUTH *come down the stairs. They walk across the hall and stop just inside the room.*

The others turn and look at them. JOEY *stands.*

TEDDY *and* RUTH *are wearing dressing-gowns.*

Silence.

TEDDY *smiles*.

                          TEDDY
Hullo . . . Dad . . . We overslept.

Pause.

What's for breakfast?

Silence.

TEDDY *chuckles*.

Huh. We overslept.

MAX *turns to* SAM.

                          MAX
Did you know he was here?

                          SAM
No.

MAX *turns to* JOEY.

                          MAX
Did you know he was here?

Pause.

I asked you if you knew he was here.

No.

Then who knew?

Pause.

Who knew?

Pause.

I didn't know.

I was going to come down, Dad, I was going to . . . be here, when you came down.

Pause.

How are you?

Pause.

Uh . . . look, I'd . . . like you to meet . . .

How long you been in this house?

All night.

MAX

All night? I'm a laughing-stock. How did you get in?

TEDDY

I had my key.

MAX *whistles and laughs.*

MAX

Who's this?

TEDDY

I was just going to introduce you.

MAX

Who asked you to bring tarts in here?

TEDDY

Tarts?

MAX

Who asked you to bring dirty tarts into this house?

TEDDY

Listen, don't be silly –

MAX

You been here all night?

TEDDY

Yes, we arrived from Venice –

MAX

We've had a smelly scrubber in my house all night.
We've had a stinking pox-ridden slut in my house all
night.

TEDDY

Stop it! What are you talking about?

MAX

I haven't seen the bitch for six years, he comes home
without a word, he brings a filthy scrubber off the
street, he shacks up in my house!

TEDDY

She's my wife! We're married!

Pause.

MAX

I've never had a whore under this roof before. Ever
since your mother died. My word of honour.
(*to* JOEY)
Have you ever had a whore here? Has Lenny ever had a
whore here? They come back from America, they bring
the slopbucket with them. They bring the bedpan with
them.
(*to* TEDDY)
Take that disease away from me. Get her away from me.

TEDDY

She's my wife.

MAX
(*to* JOEY)

Chuck them out.

Pause.

A Doctor of Philosophy, Sam, you want to meet a
Doctor of Philosophy?
(*to* JOEY)
I said chuck them out.

Pause.

What's the matter? You deaf?

JOEY

You're an old man.
(*to* TEDDY)
He's an old man.

LENNY *walks into the room, in a dressing-gown.*

He stops.

They all look round.

MAX *turns back, hits* JOEY *in the stomach with all his
might.* JOEY *contorts, staggers across the stage.* MAX,
*with the exertion of the blow, begins to collapse. His
knees buckle. He clutches his stick.*

SAM *moves forward to help him.*

MAX *hits him across the head with his stick,* SAM *sits, head in hands.*

JOEY, *hands pressed to his stomach, sinks down at the feet of* RUTH.

She looks down at him.

LENNY *and* TEDDY *are still.*

JOEY *slowly stands. He is close to* RUTH. *He turns from* RUTH, *looks round at* MAX.

SAM *clutches his head.*

MAX *breathes heavily, very slowly gets to his feet.*

JOEY *moves to him.*

They look at each other.

Silence.

MAX *moves past* JOEY, *walks towards* RUTH. *He gestures with his stick.*

                         MAX
Miss.

RUTH *walks towards him.*

                         RUTH
Yes?

68

He looks at her.

You a mother?

RUTH

Yes.

MAX

How many you got?

RUTH

Three.

He turns to TEDDY.

MAX

All yours, Ted?

Pause.

Teddy, why don't we have a nice cuddle and kiss, eh?
Like the old days? What about a nice cuddle and kiss,
eh?

TEDDY

Come on, then.

Pause.

MAX

You want to kiss your old father? Want a cuddle with
your old father?

69

Come on, then.

TEDDY moves a step towards him.

Come on.

Pause.

MAX

You still love your old Dad, eh?

They face each other.

TEDDY

Come on, Dad. I'm ready for the cuddle.

MAX begins to chuckle, gurgling.

He turns to the family and addresses them.

MAX

He still loves his father!

Curtain.

Act Two

Afternoon.

MAX, TEDDY, LENNY *and* SAM *are about the stage,
lighting cigars.*

JOEY *comes in from* U.L. *with a coffee tray, followed
by* RUTH. *He puts the tray down.* RUTH *hands coffee to
all the men. She sits with her cup.* MAX *smiles at her.*

RUTH

That was a very good lunch.

MAX

I'm glad you liked it.
                    (*to the others*)
Did you hear that?
                    (*to* RUTH)
Well, I put my heart and soul into it, I can tell you.
                    (*He sips.*)
And this is a lovely cup of coffee.

RUTH

I'm glad.

Pause.

MAX

I've got the feeling you're a first-rate cook.

71

RUTH

I'm not bad.

MAX

No, I've got the feeling you're a number one cook. Am I
right, Teddy?

TEDDY

Yes, she's a very good cook.

Pause.

MAX

Well, it's a long time since the whole family was
together, eh? If only your mother was alive. Eh, what do
you say, Sam? What would Jessie say if she was alive?
Sitting here with her three sons. Three fine grown-up
lads. And a lovely daughter-in-law. The only shame is
her grandchildren aren't here. She'd have petted them
and cooed over them, wouldn't she, Sam? She'd have
fussed over them and played with them, told them
stories, tickled them – I tell you she'd have been
hysterical.

(*to* RUTH)

Mind you, she taught those boys everything they know.
She taught them all the morality they know. I'm telling
you. Every single bit of the moral code they live by –
was taught to them by their mother. And she had a
heart to go with it. What a heart. Eh, Sam? Listen,
what's the use of beating round the bush? That woman
was the backbone to this family. I mean, I was busy
working twenty-four hours a day in the shop, I was
going all over the country to find meat, I was making

my way in the world, but I left a woman at home with a
will of iron, a heart of gold and a mind. Right, Sam?

Pause.

What a mind.

Pause.

Mind you, I was a generous man to her. I never left her
short of a few bob. I remember one year I entered into
negotiations with a top-class group of butchers with
continental connections. I was going into association
with them. I remember the night I came home, I kept
quiet. First of all I gave Lenny a bath, then Teddy a
bath, then Joey a bath. What fun we used to have in the
bath, eh, boys? Then I came downstairs and I made
Jessie put her feet up on a pouffe – what happened to
that pouffe, I haven't seen it for years – she put her feet
up on the pouffe and I said to her, Jessie, I think our
ship is going to come home. I'm going to treat you to a
couple of items, I'm going to buy you a dress in pale
corded blue silk, heavily encrusted in pearls, and for
casual wear, a pair of pantaloons in lilac flowered
taffeta. Then I gave her a drop of cherry brandy. I
remember the boys came down, in their pyjamas, all
their hair shining, their faces pink, it was before they
started shaving, and they knelt down at our feet, Jessie's
and mine. I tell you, it was like Christmas.

Pause.

73

RUTH

What happened to the group of butchers?

MAX

The group? They turned out to be a bunch of criminals like everyone else.

Pause.

This is a lousy cigar.

He stubs it out.

He turns to SAM.

What time you going to work?

SAM

Soon.

MAX

You've got a job on this afternoon, haven't you?

SAM

Yes, I know.

MAX

What do you mean, you know? You'll be late. You'll lose your job. What are you trying to do, humiliate me?

SAM

Don't worry about me.

74

MAX

It makes the bile come up in my mouth. The bile – you understand?

(*to* RUTH)

I worked as a butcher all my life, using the chopper and the slab, the slab, you know what I mean, the chopper and the slab! To keep my family in luxury. Two families! My mother was bedridden, my brothers were all invalids. I had to earn the money for the leading psychiatrists. I had to read books! I had to study the disease, so that I could cope with an emergency at every stage. A crippled family, three bastard sons, a slutbitch of a wife – don't talk to me about the pain of childbirth – I suffered the pain, I've still got the pangs – when I give a little cough my back collapses – and here I've got a lazy idle bugger of a brother won't even get to work on time. The best chauffeur in the world. All his life he's sat in the front seat giving lovely hand signals. You call that work? This man doesn't know his gearbox from his arse!

SAM

You go and ask my customers! I'm the only one they ever ask for.

MAX

What do the other drivers do, sleep all day?

SAM

I can only drive one car. They can't all have me at the same time.

MAX

Anyone could have you at the same time. You'd bend
over for half a dollar on Blackfriars Bridge.

SAM

Me!

MAX

For two bob and a toffee apple.

SAM

He's insulting me. He's insulting his brother. I'm driving
a man to Hampton Court at four forty-five.

MAX

Do you want to know who could drive? MacGregor!
MacGregor was a driver.

SAM

Don't you believe it.

MAX *points his stick at* SAM.

MAX

He didn't even fight in the war. This man didn't even
fight in the bloody war!

SAM

I did!

MAX

Who did you kill?

Silence.

SAM *gets up, goes to* RUTH, *shakes her hand and goes out of the front door.*

MAX *turns to* TEDDY.

Well, how you been keeping, son?

TEDDY
I've been keeping very well, Dad.

MAX
It's nice to have you with us, son.

TEDDY
It's nice to be back, Dad.

Pause.

MAX
You should have told me you were married, Teddy. I'd have sent you a present. Where was the wedding, in America?

TEDDY
No, here. The day before we left.

MAX
Did you have a big function?

TEDDY
No, there was no one there.

MAX

You're mad. I'd have given you a white wedding. We'd have had the cream of the cream here. I'd have been only too glad to bear the expense, my word of honour.

Pause.

TEDDY

You were busy at the time. I didn't want to bother you.

MAX

But you're my own flesh and blood. You're my first born. I'd have dropped everything. Sam would have driven you to the reception in the Snipe, Lenny would have been your best man, and then we'd have all seen you off on the boat. I mean, you don't think I disapprove of marriage, do you? Don't be daft.

(*to* RUTH)

I've been begging my two youngsters for years to find a nice feminine girl with proper credentials – it makes life worth living.

(*to* TEDDY)

Anyway, what's the difference, you did it, you made a wonderful choice, you've got a wonderful family, a marvellous career . . . so why don't we let bygones by bygones?

Pause.

You know what I'm saying? I want you both to know that you have my blessing.

TEDDY

Thank you.

MAX

Don't mention it. How many other houses in the district
have got a Doctor of Philosophy sitting down drinking
a cup of coffee?

Pause.

RUTH

I'm sure Teddy's very happy . . . to know that you're
pleased with me.

Pause.

I think he wondered whether you would be pleased
with me.

MAX

But you're a charming woman.

Pause.

RUTH

I was . . .

MAX

What?

Pause.

What she say?

79

They all look at her.

RUTH

I was . . . different . . . when I met Teddy . . . first.

TEDDY

No you weren't. You were the same.

RUTH

I wasn't.

MAX

Who cares? Listen, live in the present, what are you worrying about? I mean, don't forget the earth's about five thousand million years old, at least. Who can afford to live in the past?

Pause.

TEDDY

She's a great help to me over there. She's a wonderful wife and mother. She's a very popular woman. She's got lots of friends. It's a great life, at the University . . . you know . . . it's a very good life. We've got a lovely house . . . we've got all . . . we've got everything we want. It's a very stimulating environment.

Pause.

My department . . . is highly successful.

Pause.

We've got three boys, you know.

MAX

All boys? Isn't that funny, eh? You've got three, I've got three. You've got three nephews, Joey. Joey! You're an uncle, do you hear? You could teach them how to box.

Pause.

JOEY
(*to* RUTH)

I'm a boxer. In the evenings, after work. I'm in demolition in the daytime.

RUTH

Oh?

JOEY

Yes. I hope to be full time, when I get more bouts.

MAX
(*to* LENNY)

He speaks so easily to his sister-in-law, do you notice? That's because she's an intelligent and sympathetic woman.

He leans to her.

Eh, tell me, do you think the children are missing their mother?

She looks at him.

81

TEDDY

Of course they are. They love her. We'll be seeing them soon.

Pause.

LENNY
(*to* TEDDY)

Your cigar's gone out.

TEDDY

Oh, yes.

LENNY

Want a light?

TEDDY

No. No.

Pause.

So has yours.

LENNY

Oh, yes.

Pause.

Eh, Teddy, you haven't told us much about your Doctorship of Philosophy. What do you teach?

TEDDY

Philosophy.

LENNY

Well, I want to ask you something. Do you detect a
certain logical incoherence in the central affirmations of
Christian theism?

TEDDY

That question doesn't fall within my province.

LENNY

Well, look at it this way . . . you don't mind my asking
you some questions, do you?

TEDDY

If they're within my province.

LENNY

Well, look at it this way. How can the unknown merit
reverence? In other words, how can you revere that of
which you're ignorant? At the same time, it would be
ridiculous to propose that what we *know* merits
reverence. What we know merits any one of a number
of things, but it stands to reason reverence isn't one of
them. In other words, apart from the known and the
unknown, what else is there?

Pause.

TEDDY

I'm afraid I'm the wrong person to ask.

LENNY

But you're a philosopher. Come on, be frank. What do
you make of all this business of being and not-being?

TEDDY

What do you make of it?

LENNY

Well, for instance, take a table. Philosophically
speaking. What is it?

TEDDY

A table.

LENNY

Ah. You mean it's nothing else but a table. Well, some
people would envy your certainty, wouldn't they, Joey?
For instance, I've got a couple of friends of mine, we
often sit round the Ritz Bar having a few liqueurs, and
they're always saying things like that, you know, things
like: Take a table, take it. All right, I say, *take* it, *take* a
table, but once you've taken it, what you going to do
with it? Once you've got hold of it, where you going to
take it?

MAX

You'd probably sell it.

LENNY

You wouldn't get much for it.

JOEY

Chop it up for firewood.

LENNY *looks at him and laughs.*

84

Don't be too sure though. You've forgotten something.
Look at me. I . . . move my leg. That's all it is. But I
wear . . . underwear . . . which moves with me . . . it
. . . captures your attention. Perhaps you misinterpret.
The action is simple. It's a leg . . . moving. My lips
move. Why don't you restrict . . . your observations to
that? Perhaps the fact that they move is more significant
. . . than the words which come through them. You
must bear that . . . possibility . . . in mind.

Silence.

TEDDY *stands.*

I was born quite near here.

Pause.

Then . . . six years ago, I went to America.

Pause.

It's all rock. And sand. It stretches . . . so far . . .
everywhere you look. And there's lots of insects there.

Pause.

And there's lots of insects there.

Silence.

She is still.

MAX *stands.*

> **MAX**
> Well, it's time to go to the gym. Time for your workout,
> Joey.

> **LENNY**
> (*standing*)
> I'll come with you.

JOEY *sits looking at* RUTH.

> **MAX**
> Joe.

JOEY *stands. The three go out.*

TEDDY *sits by* RUTH, *holds her hand.*

She smiles at him.

Pause.

> **TEDDY**
> I think we'll go back. Mmnn?

Pause

Shall we go home?

> **RUTH**
> Why?

TEDDY

Well, we were only here for a few days, weren't we? We might as well . . . cut it short, I think.

RUTH

Why? Don't you like it here?

TEDDY

Of course I do. But I'd like to go back and see the boys now.

Pause.

RUTH

Don't you like your family?

TEDDY

Which family?

RUTH

Your family here.

TEDDY

Of course I like them. What are you talking about?

Pause.

RUTH

You don't like them as much as you thought you did?

TEDDY

Of course I do. Of course I . . . like them. I don't know what you're talking about.

87

Pause.

Listen. You know what time of the day it is there now, do you?

RUTH

What?

TEDDY

It's morning. It's about eleven o'clock.

RUTH

Is it?

TEDDY

Yes, they're about six hours behind us . . . I mean . . . behind the time here. The boys'll be at the pool . . . now . . . swimming. Think of it. Morning over there. Sun. We'll go anyway, mmnn? It's so clean there.

RUTH

Clean.

TEDDY

Yes.

RUTH

Is it dirty here?

TEDDY

No, of course not. But it's cleaner there.

Pause.

Look, I just brought you back to meet the family, didn't I? You've met them, we can go. The fall semester will be starting soon.

You find it dirty here?

I didn't say I found it dirty here.

Pause.

I didn't say that.

Pause.

Look. I'll go and pack. You rest for a while. Will you? They won't be back for at least an hour. You can sleep. Rest. Please.

She looks at him.

You can help me with my lectures when we get back. I'd love that. I'd be so grateful for it, really. We can bathe till October. You know that. Here, there's nowhere to bathe, except the swimming bath down the road. You know what it's like? It's like a urinal. A filthy urinal!

Pause.

You liked Venice, didn't you? It was lovely, wasn't it? You had a good week. I mean . . . I took you there. I can speak Italian.

RUTH

But if I'd been a nurse in the Italian campaign I would
have been there before.

Pause.

TEDDY

You just rest. I'll go and pack.

TEDDY *goes out and up the stairs.*

She closes her eyes.

LENNY *appears from* U.L.

He walks into the room and sits near her.

She opens her eyes.

Silence.

LENNY

Well, the evenings are drawing in.

RUTH

Yes, it's getting dark.

Pause.

LENNY

Winter'll soon be upon us. Time to renew one's
wardrobe.

Pause.

RUTH

That's a good thing to do.

LENNY

What?

Pause.

RUTH

I always . . .

Pause.

Do you like clothes?

LENNY

Oh, yes. Very fond of clothes.

Pause.

RUTH

I'm fond . . .

Pause.

What do you think of my shoes?

LENNY

They're very nice.

91

RUTH

No, I can't get the ones I want over there.

LENNY

Can't get them over there, eh?

RUTH

No . . . you don't get them there.

Pause.

I was a model before I went away.

LENNY

Hats?

Pause.

I bought a girl a hat once. We saw it in a glass case, in a shop. I tell you what it had. It had a bunch of daffodils on it, tied with a black satin bow, and then it was covered with a cloche of black veiling. A cloche. I'm telling you. She was made for it.

RUTH

No . . . I was a model for the body. A photographic model for the body.

LENNY

Indoor work?

RUTH

That was before I had . . . all my children.

92

Pause.

No, not always indoors.

Pause.

Once or twice we went to a place in the country, by train. Oh, six or seven times. We used to pass a . . . a large white water tower. This place . . . this house . . . was very big . . . the trees . . . there was a lake, you see . . . we used to change and walk down towards the lake . . . we went down a path . . . on stones . . . there were . . . on this path. Oh, just . . . wait . . . yes . . . when we changed in the house we had a drink. There was a cold buffet.

Pause.

Sometimes we stayed in the house but . . . most often . . . we walked down to the lake . . . and did our modelling there.

Pause.

Just before we went to America I went down there. I walked from the station to the gate and then I walked up the drive. There were lights on . . . I stood in the drive . . . the house was very light.

TEDDY *comes down the stairs with the cases. He puts them down, looks at* LENNY.

TEDDY

What have you been saying to her?

He goes to RUTH.

Here's your coat.

LENNY *goes to the radiogram and puts on a record of slow jazz.*

Ruth. Come on. Put it on.

LENNY
(*to* RUTH)
What about one dance before you go?

TEDDY

We're going.

LENNY

Just one.

TEDDY

No. We're going.

LENNY

Just one dance, with her brother-in-law, before she goes.

LENNY *bends to her.*

Madam?

RUTH *stands. They dance, slowly.*

94

TEDDY *stands, with* RUTH's *coat.*

MAX *and* JOEY *come in the front door and into the room. They stand.*

LENNY *kisses* RUTH. *They stand, kissing.*

JOEY

Christ, she's wide open.

Pause.

She's a tart.

Pause.

Old Lenny's got a tart in here.

JOEY *goes to them. He takes* RUTH's *arm. He smiles at* LENNY. *He sits with* RUTH *on the sofa, embraces and kisses her.*

He looks up at LENNY.

Just up my street.

He leans her back until she lies beneath him. He kisses her. He looks up at TEDDY *and* MAX.

It's better than a rubdown, this.

LENNY *sits on the arm of the sofa. He caresses* RUTH's *hair as* JOEY *embraces her.*

MAX *comes forward, looks at the cases.*

You going, Teddy? Already?

Pause.

Well, when you coming over again, eh? Look, next time you come over, don't forget to let us know beforehand whether you're married or not. I'll always be glad to meet the wife. Honest. I'm telling you.

JOEY *lies heavily on* RUTH.

They are almost still.

LENNY *caresses her hair.*

Listen, you think I don't know why you didn't tell me you were married? I know why. You were ashamed. You thought I'd be annoyed because you married a woman beneath you. You should have known me better. I'm broadminded. I'm a broadminded man.

He peers to see RUTH's *face under* JOEY, *turns back to* TEDDY.

Mind you, she's a lovely girl. A beautiful woman. And a mother too. A mother of three. You've made a happy woman out of her. It's something to be proud of. I mean, we're talking about a woman of quality. We're talking about a woman of feeling.

96

JOEY *and* RUTH *roll off the sofa on to the floor.*

JOEY *clasps her.* LENNY *moves to stand above them. He looks down on them. He touches* RUTH *gently with his foot.* RUTH *suddenly pushes* JOEY *away.*

She stands up.

JOEY *gets to his feet, stares at her.*

                    RUTH
I'd like something to eat.
                    (*to* LENNY)
I'd like a drink. Did you get any drink?

                    LENNY
We've got drink.

                    RUTH
I'd like one, please.

                    LENNY
What drink?

                    RUTH
Whisky.

                    LENNY
I've got it.

Pause.

Well, get it.

LENNY *goes to the sideboard, takes out bottle and glasses.* JOEY *moves towards her.*

Put the record off.

He looks at her, turns, puts the record off.

I want something to eat.

Pause.

JOEY

I can't cook.
                        (*pointing to* MAX)
He's the cook.

LENNY *brings her a glass of whisky.*

LENNY

Soda on the side?

RUTH

What's this glass? I can't drink out of this. Haven't you got a tumbler?

LENNY

Yes.

RUTH

Well, put it in a tumbler.

He takes the glass back, pours whisky into a tumbler, brings it to her.

LENNY

On the rocks? Or as it comes?

RUTH

Rocks? What do you know about rocks?

LENNY

We've got rocks. But they're frozen stiff in the fridge.

RUTH *drinks.*

LENNY *looks round at the others.*

Drinks all round?

He goes to the sideboard and pours drinks.

JOEY *moves closer to* RUTH.

JOEY

What food do you want?

RUTH *walks round the room.*

RUTH
(*to* TEDDY)

Has your family read your critical works?

MAX

That's one thing I've never done. I've never read one of his critical works.

TEDDY

You wouldn't understand them.

LENNY *hands drinks all round.*

JOEY

What sort of food do you want? I'm not the cook, anyway.

LENNY

Soda, Ted? Or as it comes?

TEDDY

You wouldn't understand my works. You wouldn't have the faintest idea of what they were about. You wouldn't appreciate the points of reference. You're way behind. All of you. There's no point in my sending you my works. You'd be lost. It's nothing to do with the question of intelligence. It's a way of being able to look at the world. It's a question of how far you can operate on things and not in things. I mean it's a question of your capacity to ally the two, to relate the two, to balance the two. To see, to be able to *see*! I'm the one who can see. That's why I can write my critical works. Might do you good . . . have a look at them . . . see how certain people can view . . . things . . . how certain people can maintain . . . intellectual equilibrium. Intellectual equilibrium. You're just objects. You just . . . move about. I can observe it. I can see what you do.

It's the same as I do. But you're lost in it. You won't get me being . . . I won't be lost in it.

BLACKOUT.

LIGHTS UP.

Evening.

TEDDY *sitting, in his coat, the cases by him.* SAM.

Pause.

SAM
Do you remember MacGregor, Teddy?

TEDDY
Mac?

SAM
Yes.

TEDDY
Of course I do.

SAM
What did you think of him? Did you take to him?

TEDDY
Yes. I liked him. Why?

Pause.

You know, you were always my favourite, of the lads. Always.

Pause.

When you wrote to me from America I was very touched, you know. I mean you'd written to your father a few times but you'd never written to me. But then, when I got that letter from you . . . well, I was very touched. I never told him. I never told him I'd heard from you.

Pause.

                    (*whispering*)
Teddy, shall I tell you something? You were always your mother's favourite. She told me. It's true. You were always the . . . you were always the main object of her love.

Pause.

Why don't you stay for a couple more weeks, eh? We could have a few laughs.

LENNY *comes in the front door and into the room.*

Still here, Ted? You'll be late for your first seminar.

He goes to the sideboard, opens it, peers in it, to the right and the left, stands.

Where's my cheese-roll?

Pause.

Someone's taken my cheese-roll. I left it there.
                    (*to* SAM)
You been thieving?

TEDDY

I took your cheese-roll, Lenny.

Silence.

SAM *looks at them, picks up his hat and goes out of the front door.*

Silence.

LENNY

You took my cheese-roll?

TEDDY

Yes.

LENNY

I made that roll myself. I cut it and put the butter on. I sliced a piece of cheese and put it in between. I put it on a plate and I put it in the sideboard. I did all that before I went out. Now I come back and you've eaten it.

TEDDY

Well, what are you going to do about it?

LENNY

I'm waiting for you to apologize.

TEDDY

But I took it deliberately, Lenny.

LENNY

You mean you didn't stumble on it by mistake?

TEDDY

No, I saw you put it there. I was hungry, so I ate it.

Pause.

LENNY

Barefaced audacity.

Pause.

What led you to be so . . . vindictive against your own brother? I'm bowled over.

Pause.

Well, Ted, I would say this is something approaching the naked truth, isn't it? It's a real cards on the table stunt. I mean, we're in the land of no holds barred now. Well, how else can you interpret it? To pinch your younger brother's specially made cheese-roll when he's out doing a spot of work, that's not equivocal, it's unequivocal.

Pause.

Mind you, I will say you do seem to have grown a bit sulky during the last six years. A bit sulky. A bit inner. A bit less forthcoming. It's funny, because I'd have thought that in the United States of America, I mean with the sun and all that, the open spaces, on the old campus, in your position, lecturing, in the centre of all the intellectual life out there, on the old campus, all the social whirl, all the stimulation of it all, all your kids and all that, to have fun with, down by the pool, the Greyhound buses and all that, tons of iced water, all the comfort of those Bermuda shorts and all that, on the old campus, no time of the day or night you can't get a cup of coffee or a Dutch gin, I'd have thought you'd have grown more forthcoming, not less. Because I want you to know that you set a standard for us, Teddy. Your family looks up to you, boy, and you know what it does? It does its best to follow the example you set. Because you're a great source of pride to us. That's why we were so glad to see you come back, to welcome you back to your birthplace. That's why.

Pause.

No, listen, Ted, there's no question that we live a less rich life here than you do over there. We live a closer life. We're busy, of course. Joey's busy with his boxing, I'm busy with my occupation, Dad still plays a good game of poker, and he does the cooking as well, up to his old standard, and Uncle Sam's the best chauffeur in the firm. But nevertheless we do make up a unit, Teddy, and you're an integral part of it. When we all sit round the backyard having a quiet gander at the night sky, there's always an empty chair standing in the circle,

which is in fact yours. And so when you at length
return to us, we do expect a bit of grace, a bit of je ne
sais quoi, a bit of generosity of mind, a bit of liberality
of spirit, to reassure us. We do expect that. But do we
get it? Have we got it? Is that what you've given us?

Pause.

TEDDY

Yes.

JOEY *comes down the stairs and into the room, with a
newspaper.*

LENNY
(*to* JOEY)

How'd you get on?

JOEY

Er . . . not bad.

LENNY

What do you mean?

Pause.

What do you mean?

JOEY

Not bad.

LENNY

I want to know what you *mean* – by not bad.

JOEY

What's it got to do with you?

LENNY

Joey, you tell your brother everything.

Pause.

JOEY

I didn't get all the way.

LENNY

You didn't get all the way?

Pause.
                    (*With emphasis*)
You didn't get all the way? But you've had her up there
for two hours.

JOEY

Well?

LENNY

You didn't get all the way and you've had her up there
for two hours!

JOEY

What about it?

LENNY *moves closer to him.*

LENNY

What are you telling me?

107

JOEY

What do you mean?

LENNY

Are you telling me she's a tease?

Pause.

She's a tease!

Pause.

What do you think of that, Ted? Your wife turns out to be a tease. He's had her up there for two hours and he didn't go the whole hog.

JOEY

I didn't say she was a tease.

LENNY

Are you joking? It sounds like a tease to me, don't it to you, Ted?

TEDDY

Perhaps he hasn't got the right touch.

LENNY

Joey? Not the right touch? Don't be ridiculous. He's had more dolly than you've had cream cakes. He's irresistible. He's one of the few and far between. Tell him about the last bird you had, Joey.

Pause.

JOEY

What bird?

LENNY

The last bird! When we stopped the car . . .

JOEY

Oh, that . . . yes . . . well, we were in Lenny's car one
night last week . . .

LENNY

The Alfa.

JOEY

And er . . . bowling down the road . . .

LENNY

Up near the Scrubs.

JOEY

Yes, up over by the Scrubs . . .

LENNY

We were doing a little survey of North Paddington.

JOEY

And er . . . it was pretty late, wasn't it?

LENNY

Yes, it was late. Well?

Pause.

JOEY

And then we . . . well, by the kerb, we saw this parked car . . . with a couple of girls in it.

LENNY

And their escorts.

JOEY

Yes, there were two geezers in it. Anyway . . . we got out . . . and we told the . . . two escorts . . . to go away . . . which they did . . . and then we . . . got the girls out of the car . . .

LENNY

We didn't take them over the Scrubs.

JOEY

Oh, no. Not over the Scrubs. Well, the police would have noticed us there . . . you see. We took them over a bombed site.

LENNY

Rubble. In the rubble.

JOEY

Yes, plenty of rubble.

Pause.

Well . . . you know . . . then we had them.

LENNY

You've missed out the best bit. He's missed out the best bit!

What bit?

LENNY
(*to* TEDDY)
His bird says to him, I don't mind, she says, but I've got
to have some protection. I've got to have some
contraceptive protection. I haven't got any
contraceptive protection, old Joey says to her. In that
case I won't do it, she says. Yes you will, says Joey,
never mind about the contraceptive protection.

LENNY *laughs*.

Even my bird laughed when she heard that. Yes, even
she gave out a bit of a laugh. So you can't say old Joey
isn't a bit of a knockout when he gets going, can you?
And here he is upstairs with your wife for two hours
and he hasn't even been the whole hog. Well, your wife
sounds like a bit of a tease to me, Ted. What do you
make of it, Joey? You satisfied? Don't tell me you're
satisfied without going the whole hog?

Pause.

JOEY
I've been the whole hog plenty of times. Sometimes . . .
you can be happy . . . and not go the whole hog. Now
and again . . . you can be happy . . . without going any
hog.

LENNY *stares at him.*

MAX *and* SAM *come in the front door and into the room.*

MAX

Where's the whore? Still in bed? She'll make us all animals.

LENNY

The girl's a tease.

MAX

What?

LENNY

She's had Joey on a string.

MAX

What do you mean?

TEDDY

He had her up there for two hours and he didn't go the whole hog.

Pause.

MAX

My Joey? She did that to my boy?

Pause.

To my youngest son? Tch, tch, tch, tch. How you feeling, son? Are you all right?

JOEY

Sure I'm all right.

MAX
(*to* TEDDY)

Does she do that to you, too?

TEDDY

No.

LENNY

He gets the gravy.

MAX

You think so?

JOEY

No he don't.

Pause.

SAM

He's her lawful husband. She's his lawful wife.

JOEY

No he don't! He don't get no gravy! I'm telling you. I'm telling all of you. I'll kill the next man who says he gets the gravy.

MAX

Joey . . . what are you getting so excited about?
(*to* LENNY)

It's because he's frustrated. You see what happens?

Who is?

MAX

Joey. No one's saying you're wrong. In fact everyone's saying you're right.

Pause.

MAX *turns to the others.*

You know something? Perhaps it's not a bad idea to have a woman in the house. Perhaps it's a good thing. Who knows? Maybe we should keep her.

Pause.

Maybe we'll ask her if she wants to stay.

Pause.

TEDDY

I'm afraid not, Dad. She's not well, and we've got to get home to the children.

MAX

Not well? I told you, I'm used to looking after people who are not so well. Don't worry about that. Perhaps we'll keep her here.

Pause.

SAM

Don't be silly.

MAX

What's silly?

SAM

You're talking rubbish.

MAX

Me?

SAM

She's got three children.

MAX

She can have more! Here. If she's so keen.

TEDDY

She doesn't want any more.

MAX

What do you know about what she wants, eh, Ted?

TEDDY
(*smiling*)

The best thing for her is to come home with me, Dad. Really. We're married, you know.

MAX *walks about the room clicks his fingers.*

MAX

We'd have to pay her, of course. You realize that? We

can't leave her walking about without any pocket
money. She'll have to have a little allowance.

JOEY

Of course we'll pay her. She's got to have some money
in her pocket.

MAX

That's what I'm saying. You can't expect a woman to
walk about without a few bob to spend on a pair of
stockings.

Pause.

LENNY

Where's the money going to come from?

MAX

Well, how much is she worth? What we talking about,
three figures?

LENNY

I asked you where the money's going to come from. It'll
be an extra mouth to feed. It'll be an extra body to
clothe. You realize that?

JOEY

I'll buy her clothes.

LENNY

What with?

JOEY

I'll put in a certain amount out of my wages.

MAX

That's it. We'll pass the hat round. We'll make a
donation. We're all grown-up people, we've got a sense
of responsibility. We'll all put a little in the hat. It's
democratic.

LENNY

It'll come to a few quid, Dad.

Pause.

I mean, she's not a woman who likes walking around in
second-hand goods. She's up to the latest fashion. You
wouldn't want her walking about in clothes which don't
show her off at her best, would you?

MAX

Lenny, do you mind if I make a little comment? It's not
meant to be critical. But I think you're concentrating
too much on the economic considerations. There are
other considerations. There are the human
considerations. You understand what I mean? There are
the human considerations. Don't forget them.

LENNY

I won't.

MAX

Well don't.

Pause.

Listen, we're bound to treat her in something approximating, at least, to the manner in which she's accustomed. After all, she's not someone off the street, she's my daughter-in-law!

JOEY

That's right.

MAX

There you are, you see. Joey'll donate, Sam'll donate . . .

SAM *looks at him.*

I'll put a few bob out of my pension, Lenny'll cough up. We're laughing. What about you, Ted? How much you going to put in the kitty?

TEDDY

I'm not putting anything in the kitty.

MAX

What? You won't even help to support your own wife? You lousy stinkpig. Your mother would drop dead if she heard you take that attitude.

LENNY

Eh, Dad.

LENNY *walks forward.*

I've got a better idea.

What?

There's no need for us to go to all this expense. I know
these women. Once they get started they ruin your
budget. I've got a better idea. Why don't I take her up
with me to Greek Street?

Pause.

You mean put her on the game?

Pause.

We'll put her on the game. That's a stroke of genius,
that's a marvellous idea. You mean she can earn the
money herself – on her back?

Yes.

Wonderful. The only thing is, it'll have to be short
hours. We don't want her out of the house all night.

I can limit the hours.

MAX

How many?

LENNY

Four hours a night.

MAX

(*dubiously*)

Is that enough?

LENNY

She'll bring in a good sum for four hours a night.

MAX

Well, you should know. After all, it's true, the last thing
we want to do is wear the girl out. She's going to have
her obligations this end as well. Where you going to put
her in Greek Street?

LENNY

It doesn't have to be right in Greek Street, Dad. I've got
a number of flats all around that area.

MAX

You have? Well, what about me? Why don't you give
me one?

LENNY

You're sexless.

JOEY

Eh, wait a minute, what's all this?

MAX

I know what Lenny's saying. Lenny's saying she can pay her own way. What do you think, Teddy? That'll solve all our problems.

JOEY

Eh, wait a minute. I don't want to share her.

MAX

What did you say?

JOEY

I don't want to share her with a lot of yobs!

MAX

Yobs! You arrogant git! What arrogance.
(*to* LENNY)
Will you be supplying her with yobs?

LENNY

I've got a very distinguished clientele, Joey. They're more distinguished than you'll ever be.

MAX

So you can count yourself lucky we're including you in.

JOEY

I didn't think I was going to have to share her!

MAX

Well, you *are* going to have to share her! Otherwise she goes straight back to America. You understand?

Pause.

It's tricky enough as it is, without you shoving your oar in. But there's something worrying me. Perhaps she's not so up to the mark. Eh? Teddy, you're the best judge. Do you think she'd be up to the mark?

Pause.

I mean what about all this teasing? Is she going to make a habit of it? That'll get us nowhere.

Pause.

TEDDY

It was just love play . . . I suppose . . . that's all I suppose it was.

MAX

Love play? Two bleeding hours? That's a bloody long time for love play!

LENNY

I don't think we've got anything to worry about on that score, Dad.

MAX

How do you know?

LENNY

I'm giving you a professional opinion.

LENNY *goes to* TEDDY.

LENNY

Listen, Teddy, you could help us, actually. If I were to
send you some cards, over to America . . . you know,
very nice ones, with a name on, and a telephone
number, very discreet, well, you could distribute them
. . . to various parties, who might be making a trip over
here. Of course, you'd get a little percentage out of it.

MAX

I mean, you needn't tell them she's your wife.

LENNY

No, we'd call her something else. Dolores, or
something.

MAX

Or Spanish Jacky.

LENNY

No, you've got to be reserved about it, Dad. We could
call her something nice . . . like Cynthia . . . or Gillian.

Pause.

JOEY

Gillian.

Pause.

LENNY

No, what I mean, Teddy, you must know lots of
professors, heads of departments, men like that. They
pop over here for a week at the Savoy, they need

somewhere they can go to have a nice quiet poke. And of course you'd be in a position to give them inside information.

MAX

Sure. You can give them proper data. I bet you before two months we'd have a waiting list.

LENNY

You could be our representative in the States.

MAX

Of course. We're talking in international terms! By the time we've finished Pan-American'll give us a discount.

Pause.

TEDDY

She'd get old . . . very quickly.

MAX

No . . . not in this day and age! With the health service? Old! How could she get old? She'll have the time of her life.

RUTH *comes down the stairs, dressed.*

She comes into the room.

She smiles at the gathering, and sits.

Silence.

124

TEDDY

Ruth . . . the family have invited you to stay, for a little while longer. As a . . . as a kind of guest. If you like the idea I don't mind. We can manage very easily at home . . . until you come back.

RUTH

How very nice of them.

Pause.

MAX

It's an offer from our heart.

RUTH

It's very sweet of you.

MAX

Listen . . . it would be our pleasure.

Pause.

RUTH

I think I'd be too much trouble.

MAX

Trouble? What are you talking about? What trouble? Listen, I'll tell you something. Since poor Jessie died, eh, Sam? we haven't had a woman in the house. Not one. Inside this house. And I'll tell you why. Because their mother's image was so dear any other woman would have . . . tarnished it. But you . . . Ruth . . . you're not

only lovely and beautiful, but you're kin. You're kith.
You belong here.

Pause.

RUTH

I'm very touched.

MAX

Of course you're touched. I'm touched.

Pause.

TEDDY

But Ruth, I should tell you . . . that you'll have to pull
your weight a little, if you stay. Financially. My father
isn't very well off.

RUTH
(*to* MAX)

Oh, I'm sorry.

MAX

No, you'd just have to bring in a little, that's all. A few
pennies. Nothing much. It's just that we're waiting for
Joey to hit the top as a boxer. When Joey hits the top
. . . well . . .

Pause.

TEDDY

Or you can come home with me.

LENNY

We'd get you a flat.

Pause.

RUTH

A flat?

LENNY

Yes.

RUTH

Where?

LENNY

In town.

Pause.

But you'd live here, with us.

MAX

Of course you would. This would be your home. In the bosom of the family.

LENNY

You'd just pop up to the flat a couple of hours a night, that's all.

MAX

Just a couple of hours, that's all. That's all.

LENNY

And you make enough money to keep you going here.

Pause.

RUTH

How many rooms would this flat have?

LENNY

Not many.

RUTH

I would want at least three rooms and a bathroom.

LENNY

You wouldn't need three rooms and a bathroom.

MAX

She'd need a bathroom.

LENNY

But not three rooms.

Pause.

RUTH

Oh, I would. Really.

LENNY

Two would do.

RUTH

No. Two wouldn't be enough.

128

Pause.

I'd want a dressing-room, a rest-room, and a bedroom.

Pause.

LENNY

All right, we'll get you a flat with three rooms and a bathroom.

RUTH

With what kind of conveniences?

LENNY

All conveniences.

RUTH

A personal maid?

LENNY

Of course.

Pause.

We'd finance you, to begin with, and then, when you were established, you could pay us back, in instalments.

RUTH

Oh, no, I wouldn't agree to that.

LENNY

Oh, why not?

RUTH

You would have to regard your original outlay simply
as a capital investment.

Pause.

LENNY

I see. All right.

RUTH

You'd supply my wardrobe, of course?

LENNY

We'd supply everything. Everything you need.

RUTH

I'd need an awful lot. Otherwise I wouldn't be content.

LENNY

You'd have everything.

RUTH

I would naturally want to draw up an inventory of
everything I would need, which would require your
signatures in the presence of witnesses.

LENNY

Naturally.

RUTH

All aspects of the agreement and conditions of
employment would have to be clarified to our mutual
satisfaction before we finalized the contract.

LENNY

Of course.

Pause.

RUTH

Well, it might prove a workable arrangement.

LENNY

I think so.

MAX

And you'd have the whole of your daytime free, of
course. You could do a bit of cooking here if you
wanted to.

LENNY

Make the beds.

MAX

Scrub the place out a bit.

TEDDY

Keep everyone company.

SAM *comes forward.*

SAM
(*in one breath*)

MacGregor had Jessie in the back of my cab as I drove
them along.

He croaks and collapses.

131

He lies still.

They look at him.

MAX

What's he done? Dropped dead?

LENNY

Yes.

MAX

A corpse? A corpse on my floor? Get him out of here!
Clear him out of here!

JOEY *bends over* SAM.

JOEY

He's not dead.

LENNY

He probably was dead, for about thirty seconds.

MAX

He's not even dead!

LENNY *looks down at* SAM.

LENNY

Yes, there's still some breath there.

MAX
(*pointing at* SAM)
You know what that man had?

LENNY

Has.

MAX

Has! A diseased imagination.

Pause.

RUTH

Yes, it sounds a very attractive idea.

MAX

Do you want to shake on it now, or do you want to
leave it till later?

RUTH

Oh, we'll leave it till later.

TEDDY *stands.*

He looks down at SAM.

TEDDY

I was going to ask him to drive me to London Airport.

He goes to the cases, picks one up.

Well, I'll leave your case, Ruth. I'll just go up the road
to the Underground.

MAX

Listen, if you go the other way, first left, first right, you
remember, you might find a cab passing there.

TEDDY

Yes, I might do that.

MAX

Or you can take the tube to Piccadilly Circus, won't take you ten minutes, and pick up a cab from there out to the Airport.

TEDDY

Yes, I'll probably do that.

MAX

Mind you, they'll charge you double fare. They'll charge you for the return trip. It's over the six-mile limit.

TEDDY

Yes. Well, bye-bye, Dad. Look after yourself.

They shake hands.

MAX

Thanks, son. Listen. I want to tell you something. It's been wonderful to see you.

Pause.

TEDDY

It's been wonderful to see you.

MAX

Do your boys know about me? Eh? Would they like to see a photo, do you think, of their grandfather?

134

I know they would.

MAX *brings out his wallet.*

MAX
I've got one on me. I've got one here. Just a minute.
Here you are. Will they like that one?

TEDDY
(taking it)
They'll be thrilled.

He turns to LENNY.

Good-bye, Lenny.

They shake hands.

LENNY
Ta-ta, Ted. Good to see you. Have a good trip.

TEDDY
Bye-bye, Joey.

JOEY *does not move.*

JOEY
Ta-ta.

TEDDY *goes to the front door.*

RUTH
Eddie.

TEDDY *turns.*

Pause.

Don't become a stranger.

TEDDY *goes, shuts the front door.*

Silence.

The three men stand.

RUTH *sits relaxed on her chair.*

SAM *lies still.*

JOEY *walks slowly across the room.*

He kneels at her chair.

She touches his head, lightly.

He puts his head in her lap.

MAX *begins to move above them, backwards and forwards.*

LENNY *stands still.*

MAX *turns to* LENNY.

MAX
I'm too old, I suppose. She thinks I'm an old man.

Pause.

I'm not such an old man.

Pause.

(*to* RUTH)
You think I'm too old for you?

Pause.

Listen. You think you're just going to get that big slag
all the time? You think you're just going to have him
. . . you're going to just have him all the time? You're
going to have to work! You'll have to take them on, you
understand?

Pause.

Does she realize that?

Pause.

Lenny, do you think she understands . . .

He begins to stammer.

Wait . . . what . . . what . . . we're getting at? What . . .
we've got in mind? Do you think she's got it clear?

Pause.

I don't think she's got it clear.

137

Pause.

You understand what I mean? Listen, I've got a funny idea she'll do the dirty on us, you want to bet? She'll use us, she'll make use of us, I can tell you! I can smell it! You want to bet?

Pause.

She won't . . . be adaptable!

He begins to groan, clutches his stick, falls on to his knees by the side of her chair. His body sags. The groaning stops. His body straightens. He looks at her, still kneeling.

I'm not an old man.

Pause.

Do you hear me?

He raises his face to her.

Kiss me.

She continues to touch JOEY'S *head, lightly.*

LENNY *stands, watching.*

Curtain.